# The Power of Persuasion

*Understand the Psychology of Persuasion, Influence Human Behavior, and Get Others to Do What You Want*

Henrik Rodgers

# Table of Contents

# Introduction

If you want to succeed in life at some level or another, and regardless of your industry, profession, location, age, gender or any other aspect, you have to become more persuasive, you need to influence people what you want them to do.

Let's put it straight that persuasion is not some alien or a completely foreign body of knowledge... If you look at what you're doing in the course of a day, chances are, you are already doing it. You might not be all that successful with it currently, but you are already doing it.

In fact, persuasion is rooted in daily communication. For example, you're going to ask people to do stuff for you. Maybe you're negotiating at a fairly low level every single day. Even if you ask for a better price or if you're asking for more stuff with your order, you are negotiating. When you negotiate, you are trying to persuade the other person to do what you'd like them to do.

Persuasion is nothing but an active attempt of changing another person's attitudes, beliefs, or behavior about anything – it's a form of social influence through triggering human psychology. To be clear, persuasion is not manipulation. Manipulation is when someone has a negative influence on someone else by using unethical means, like intentionally lying to them.

In fact, persuasion is a key part of our daily communications. The problem? We settle for less than optimal results when we try to persuade. We think that we can't improve this part of our skill set. We think that we're doing the best we can, and whatever we get is pretty much the best we could hope for. It is no surprise that too many people settle for service quality and product quality that is below what they deserve. People only give us the most basic deals, services and considerations.

But in reality, there are few tiny but effective psychological triggers that can significantly enhance the probability of you getting whatever you want from the other person. You need to be aware about those triggers and then use those triggers effectively to get the results.

Let's understand this trigger effect with the help of an example. There is a psychological tactic of starting with a little request in order to get an eventually larger compliance from people- known as **foot-in-the-door** technique.

There was a study conducted in 1960s. The home-owners in some residential area of California were approached by the researchers by knocking door after door and make a huge request to residents. The homeowners were asked to allow the research install a public service billboard on their front lawn. The researchers showed the imagery depiction of how their house would look like after putting the billboard- in effect after putting the billboard, the view of the house would completely get obscured by a very large, and poorly lettered signed stating "DRIVE CAREFULLY". People understood the request and a whopping majority of 83% people simple refused to put the billboard. But something interesting happened in another nearby residential area, where 76% people agreed to put such a big billboard obscuring the view of their house.

How did that happen? Why only a meager 17% people agreed in one area, while on the other hand a mass majority of 76% people gave their consent for putting the billboard.

Let me pull the curtain. The key reason for this astonishing compliance on part of people was another small experiment that was conducted 2 weeks before. Another volunteer worker had visited these homeowners and asked them to accept and display a small 3 inches square sign that read "BE A SAFE DRIVER" on the main door. This request appeared so trivial to people that most of them agreed to put that small sign. But the effect of agreeing to small request was tremendous in terms of agreeing to a much bigger request later.

The research had in fact revealed this psychological trait of humans; people who had innocently agreed to a small request, later on became willing to comply with a much bigger request. Making people agree to put a smaller sign board was the practical application of foot-in-the-door technique that later led to a getting people to agree to a bigger compliance. Once people get committed to something, they generally want to stay consistent in that approach. 76% compliant group did agree to bigger billboard as a measure of commitment and consistency to their approach as safety conscious citizens. Moral of the story – to change a behavior, get your foot in the door.

Now, please understand that persuasion takes place not just in commercial transactions, but in your relationships as well. When you're doing any kind of communication, chances are, you are settling for far less than you deserve.

Unfortunately, a lot of people are clueless about the fact that they could get more. That's right, they could maximize whatever benefits they're already getting from their interpersonal interactions. Please understand that this is not selfishness. This is not manipulation. This is not evil. Instead, it's all about increasing your ability to persuade others and it is all about being a more effective human being. In fact, you're just being responsible if you hone your persuasion skills. You owe it to yourself.

If you are in any way unhappy or frustrated with whatever results life is giving you, maybe you'd want to hone your persuasion skills. By doing so, maybe you'll get a lot more out of your personal interactions.

There's a lot of give and take in life. And unfortunately, if we neglect or overlook our ability to persuade, then chances are, we may not get the very best of most bargains we get into. But if you pay attention and learn this important skill, you generate the ability to produce a distinct kind of automatic and mindless compliance from people – means people become willing to say yes without thinking first. And that's what persuasion is all about- getting people to do what you want by applying some triggers.

## How This Book Will Help You?

In this book, you will learn how becoming more persuasive can tremendously improve your personal, financial, social life and relationship with other people. If you've been ignoring this important skill under some myth by calling it manipulating or cheating people, you'll learn how misconceived your beliefs have been so far, and what you've already lost and will continue to lose, if you don't change your approach.

The most important part, you'll learn numerous effective techniques about how to use your body language, how to build trust by effective story-telling and become more likeable amongst people, so you can generate the desired results from your interactions.

You'll understand how you can become comfortable with yourself and with the people around, and thus build strong persuasion muscles. All in all, by the end of this book, you'll find yourself equipped with practical, actionable and effective principles and tactics to unleash the power of persuasion and ready to transform the quality of your life.

Now let's get started.

# Chapter 1: What Exactly Do You Gain?

If you were to increase your ability to persuade other human beings, what exactly do you stand to gain? What are the broad parameters of life improvement that you should look for?

Please understand that whenever you interact with other people, there is always a possibility of mutual gain or mutual loss. In most cases, people settle for a win-loss situation. They lose a little bit, somebody gains a lot more. Some people settle for a little bit of a win, and the other person walks away with the lion's share of benefits.

It doesn't have to be that way. The first step to becoming more persuasive is to get a clear idea of what exactly you stand to gain. By being clear on the benefits of this skill, you can then get the focus and motivation you need to work on it.

**Get People to Say "Yes"**

Are you the type of person who always gets the answer "no" or "maybe?" it can get really irritating and it can get old really quickly. Unfortunately, too many of us believe that this is the best we can do. In fact, some people are under the impression that this is the best they could hope for.

This is not true. Just because you have asked for something repeatedly over an extended period of time and the answer always comes out "no" or "maybe," it doesn't necessarily mean that's all there is. Maybe if you were able to persuade them, you would get a lot more "yes" answers.

Let's put it this way, just because you have been denied for so long, it doesn't necessarily mean that the answer to all your needs is a resounding "no." When you practice your ability to persuade others, you get more people to say "yes." Of course, nobody can guarantee that they will always say "yes." But you will definitely be able to get "yes" answers more often than before.

## Get Others to Unite Around a Common Goal

Are you the type of person who simply joins groups after they have made up their mind? Are you the one who just goes along to get along long after the group's decision has been made? Wouldn't it be nice to be the person who actually rallies everybody else to achieve more together?

If any of these questions have ever entered your mind, part of your frustration lies in the fact that you're not a very persuasive person.

You have to understand that when people gather together, there are certain needs and problems that unite them. These needs can actually be expressed and articulated in a way that it creates a common goal that unites everybody. The reality is that with the right leadership, when people get together, they will be able to achieve far more than what they would normally be able to do by themselves. This is the power of groups.

If you think you're smart, resourceful and capable, can you imagine if there is 20, 100, or even 1,000 of you? Can you imagine the possibilities? When you cultivate your ability to persuade others, you would be able to get others to see their common problems and unite around a common solution to achieve a common goal. This boosts your organic levels of leadership, and this enables you to benefit from the products of everybody's efforts.

## Be More Attractive

Believe or not, if you are a persuasive person, people are more likely to overlook your physical limitations. In fact, in many cases, many women prefer guys who are simply socially magnetic. They may not be all that attractive, they may not be easy on the eyes, but none of that matters.

Why? They carry so much clout with the people around them that they make things happen.

When you hone your ability to persuade others, you become more powerful. You're able to leverage other people's strengths to produce results. Not everybody can do that. And if you are able to communicate this clearly, you become more attractive to members of the opposite sex as well.

## Be More Magnetic

When you're in a group, it's very easy for people to compete with each other. It's very easy for egos to collide. Accordingly, it's easy for less persuasive and less charismatic people to basically be pushed towards the back of the group.

This has a serious implication on how much money they make, how much respect they command, and how high up they go in any kind of social hierarchy. When you master the art of persuasion, you become more magnetic.

Most people are sheep. Seriously. Most people are sheep looking for shepherds. They're looking to be led. Most people would rather procrastinate. In fact, on many levels, people are lazy. When you come off as a person who has a goal or a direction or a purpose, people are naturally attracted towards that. But the thing that seals the deal is your ability to get everybody else to sign off on your personal vision. Such people are magnetic. If you need an example of this, look at the career of Steve Jobs or Apple Computers. These are people with a vision.

Now, the vision doesn't have to be world changing, it doesn't have to necessarily be revolutionary, but as long as you have a vision and you're able to get people to emotionally become invested in that vision, you stand apart from everybody else.

The vast majority of people are lazy, unmotivated and are only focused on what's two feet in front of them. This is why they're almost automatically drawn to people who have vision and who are able to communicate and persuade others about that vision.

## Inspire Others to Pull Their Strengths to Overcome Impossible Odds

If you have ever seen college football movies, you must have noticed that in many of these movies, the heroes of the movie are in a team who are facing impossible odds. For whatever reason, it seems that they are dead in the water.

Anybody in their right minds would just have given up a long time ago. However, either the coach or one of the players is able to inspire everybody else to look deep within themselves and find the strength they need to overcome their fears.

It doesn't matter what the odds are, it doesn't matter what they're up against, when that central person persuades everybody else to go through this self analysis to find the inner core strength they need to push back and eventually overcome, you can't help but cheer for that team. It resonates with you at a very deep level.

You can be that person. Instead of waiting around for such a heroic person to appear, you can be that person by simply investing your time, focus and energy on becoming more persuasive.

**Make More Money**

That's right, if you're a persuasive person, you can make more money. You have to understand that there are a lot of people on this planet ready and eager to hand you their money. There's only one problem. You have to give them a good reason.

This is why sales people are focused less on technical details. Instead, they focus more on reading the signals that the prospect is sending them so they can say the right things at the right time to make the right impression to seal the deal. This requires persuasion. And if you're able to do that repeatedly with many different clients, different audiences and different customers, you make more and more money.

You have to understand that the true nature of money is that it is a vote of value. That's all it is. Money, in and of itself, has no intrinsic value. It's just something that we all collectively agree will store value.

When you look at how value is created, passed on, pulled, and otherwise mobilized, it should become clear to you that the secret to unlocking how money is directed is persuasion. For example, if you're able to persuade web development customers that your web design company is worth $10,000 an hour, you're going to make that much money. On the other hand, if you can't persuade them to pay you that amount of money, it doesn't matter how awesome your past work is and how highly regarded you are in your industry. People are not going to pony up and give you that cash.

Because that's how markets work. Markets don't care how much blood, sweat and tears you put into your product. If you are unable to persuade market players to buy from you at a certain price, your work has less value. Your value relies primarily on how well you can persuade the buyer to pay for your work. I hope this much is clear.

Again, it doesn't matter how much raw resources, labor, time, sweat and blood you put into a product, if the market says it's $5, it's $5. Unless, of course, you can persuade your buyers to pay more. And this is where branding comes in.

Make no mistake, Nike sneakers can be manufactured in China and Vietnam at a cost of only few dollars. But the moment you put on the Nike swoosh logo on those shoes, the price goes up to north of $200. Do you see how that works?

Branding is persuasion. You're basically telling the buyer, "You're not buying shoes. You're buying a brand. When you buy the Nike brand, you buy a lifestyle. You buy a piece of sportswear history."

Now, you have to get people to believe that. And that belief comes with a cost. You have to understand that there's quite a big cost difference between $5 and $200 or more. Master persuasion and you are sure to make more money.

## Command More Respect

People who are able to convince others to see eye to eye with them and agree with their position are very powerful people. It doesn't matter whether you have the "truth" on your side, if nobody believes you, you are powerless. Understand this.

Finding the truth and basing your life on it are only initial steps. You have to communicate clearly and persuade others. Otherwise, you're going to be left at a serious disadvantage.

The more persuasive you are, the more respect you command from others. Respect can turn into higher pay, it can turn into greater sexual selection in terms of partners, it can be converted into power, it can be converted into social position, you name it. But to generate respect, you have to be persuasive.

Precisely, life becomes pretty exciting if you have developed persuasion muscle because you are confident that you can get people do what you want them to do. Now let's move to next chapter and see how badly people suffer if they are totally unpersuasive.

# Chapter 2: How Bad Can It Get If You are Totally Unpersuasive?

I've added this chapter into this book because there are two types of people: proactive and reactive. If you are a proactive person, you are motivated primarily by what you stand to gain. When you hope, wish and dream about attaining something, you get pumped up. You get motivated.

Unfortunately, most of us are not proactive. Most of us would only lift a finger to change our situation when we notice that our backs are against the wall and we're in the fourth quarter of the basketball game with only 30 seconds left on the clock. A lot of us choose to react rather than take proactive action about the big things in our lives.

To address reactive individuals, I'm going to focus now on what you stand to lose if you are totally unpersuasive. Being persuasive or not being persuasive is not merely a yes or no game, it's double whammy – while you gain immensely by learning persuasion skills; but you lose miserable if you don't pay attention to this important life skills. If you're not motivated enough by what you stand to gain as you learned in the previous chapter, pay attention to what you stand to lose.

## You Waste Whatever Talents and Skills You Have

If you're not persuasive, it doesn't matter if you are the smartest guy in the room. Seriously. It doesn't matter if you are extremely creative and you are the second coming of Michelangelo. You will always be underrated, under-appreciated, underpaid and underdeveloped.

Whatever resources the organization you're a part of may possess, very little of it will go to you. Instead, it might be wasted on other people who are less talented and less intelligent than you.

But guess what? It won't matter because they do such a better job of persuading others regarding their value. You will get left behind. You will get passed over for promotions. You will get overlooked and taken for granted.

## You are Unable to Achieve Key Parts of Your Life's Purpose

All of us are on this planet for a reason. We all have a life purpose. Now, unfortunately, the vast majority of us live our live in such a way that it seems that life is meaningless and purposeless. People are entitled to live their lives that way, but this fact in no way takes away from the reality that we have a life purpose. We only experience the power of that purpose when we choose to be aware of that purpose in the first place.

But the reality is that you can choose your life's purpose. That's right. You're not doomed to repeat some script that your parents lived. Just because you come from a certain group of people, it doesn't mean that you are cursed with their collective destiny. No. You can choose your life's purpose.

But here's the problem, if you are an unpersuasive person, you will not be able to unlock certain parts of your life's purpose. You know that that's what you are born to do, but because you have neglected your ability to persuade others, they remain far away.

There's nothing more depressing than living life day to day knowing that there's a higher purpose for you. Unfortunately, you feel like you're stuck where you are. You know that you're capable of so much more, but here you are, living a mediocre life.

## You Work Twice as Hard to Get the Same Results

If you're the type of person who is a go-getter and puts in a lot of energy to your daily tasks and daily objectives only to get disappointing results, it may be because you invested your time in the wrong things.

Now, don't me wrong, you should invest your time in knowledge. Technical knowledge can go a long way. You should also invest your time in insight and wisdom. Those are good things.

But the problem is, success is not just defined by the things that we do on our own. Most of the time, for us to achieve big things in life, we have to rely on other people. We have to plug into some sort of social system. And that's why you need to be more persuasive.

As talented, skilled and creative as you may be, if you are unable to persuade others to work towards your goals or to assist you in achieving your big objectives, you're going to continue to struggle. As the old saying goes, no man is an island. You need to start building bridges, but those bridges are built with the concrete of persuasion.

## You Fail to Tap the Power of Brainstorming and Synergy

There's a saying, two heads are better than one, precisely because when you put two heads together, you don't just put one plus one to arrive at two. You actually get exponential results.

When you're brainstorming and you're looking for opportunities with other business people, amazing success can be had when you are able to persuade them to become emotionally and intellectually invested in your vision. You have to understand that visionaries can only go so far. They can only see the broad outlines, but everybody else has to fill in the details.

Steve Jobs can see that mobile computing devices are the future. Jonathan Ive, the head designer of Apple, filled in the rest of the picture and out came the iPhone, the iPod and the iPad. The same applies to you. You may have all these great ideas inspired by your experiences and technical know-how, but you need to communicate them in such a way that they inspire others to fill in the rest of the picture.

That's how you create synergy. And a little bit of synergy can go a long way to produce amazing success.

## You Always Feel Like an Outsider

Do you ever get the feeling that when you're in a group of people that people can't seem to understand you? Do you often struggle with communication issues? It seems that no matter how much you talk, people still can't fully get what you're about.

Welcome to the club. A lot of people actually settle for less than satisfactory social lives precisely because they neglected their ability to persuade others.

You have to understand that a core component of persuasion is clear communication. It's easy to feel like an outsider when people routinely misunderstand you or they seem to listen to you up to a certain point. Past that point, they're completely deaf to you.

Now, please understand that this is happening not because they have something against you. This happens usually because you do not communicate at their level. You're not able to get the idea from your head and your heart to their heads and their hearts in an effective and clear way. You need persuasion for that.

## You Feel a Frustrating Sense of Disconnection

Do you often feel disconnected to people? It seems like regardless of how much time you spend with others, you really can't quite see eye to eye. There is some sort of emotional or intellectual disconnect or both. A lot of people suffer from this problem because they are unable to communicate in a persuasive way.

You have to understand that there are many things in life that you need to talk people into. Things may seem black and white from your perspective, but don't assume for a second that everybody would agree that things look that cut and dried. Often times, things look very different from their perspective.

This should not be a surprise. Everybody comes from different backgrounds, have different experiences, and deal with different emotional complications. You have to communicate in such a way that overrides all of that. And that's where persuasion comes in.

Make no mistake, if you are totally unpersuasive, you end up wasting your life. You may have a lot of love to give, you may be a very resourceful, imaginative and creative person, you may have really amazing insights and a powerful sense of intuition, but let me tell you, if you neglect your personal power of persuasion, almost all of that goes to waste.

The only person that gets to enjoy them is you. But unfortunately, you'll be enjoying them pretty much alone. The more persuasive you are, the more you draw people into your circle.

As Stephen Covey stated there are three levels of human growth. We start with first level called 'dependence'- means we start our life by depending on others. As a kid we are dependent emotionally, physically, mentally and financially on our parents. But as we grow up, we aim for independence in every area – so the second stage is 'independence'. Though most people don't get independent in all the above areas of life, but that's a different story for the other day.  But most people stop there under a belief that they can now get the best out of life by just becoming independent. But that's far from truth; you can't go much far with this approach. Because there is one apex level called 'inter-dependence', where you co-ordinate, synergize with other people, and then you start getting the benefits of collective wisdom, insights and massive action of many people moving towards the bigger common purpose. And you cannot move up to the stage of 'inter-dependence', unless you have persuasion skills.

Hope these chapters clarify the immense potential of persuasion and now you are ready to master the art of persuasion, so let's get into the next chapter for that.

# Chapter 3: 7 Steps To Mastering the Art of Persuasion

In this book, I'm going to teach you a practical series of steps and clusters of techniques that would enable you to increase your power of persuasion.

Now, at this point, I don't want you to walk away with the impression that if you've read all these materials that all of a sudden you would be the master persuader. I don't want the idea to get into your head that almost overnight you will be able to talk anybody and everybody in any kind of situation to do whatever you want them to do. Maybe you will get to that level at some point in time, but not overnight.

Instead, you should just focus on achieving some incremental improvements in your current level of persuasion. Maybe this would lead to more people doing favors for you. Maybe this would lead to you getting slightly better prices or people giving you slightly more benefit of the doubt.

Whatever the case may be, adopt an initial incremental view. Don't expect some sort of black and white transformation from a completely unpersuasive and disconnected person to being the center of the show. I mean, I'm sure that happens, but at this point, you need to manage your expectations so as not to set yourself up for discouragement.

If you're getting into this with the expectation that after you read this book you will automatically become salesman of the year in your company, you're setting yourself up for a big letdown. Oftentimes, it doesn't work that way. But you will enjoy improvements.

The problem is, if you set yourself up with such high expectations, any sort of discouragement may be enough for you to stop working on your persuasion abilities. Don't do that. Be realistic with your expectations and position yourself for long lasting success.

**The Steps to Increased Levels of Persuasion**

This book will teach you the following skills so you can become a more persuasive person:

- Learn to get comfortable
- Understand the power of body language
- Get people around you to become more comfortable
- Learn to build trust
- Use the art of likeability
- Benefit from social proof
- Learn how to pre-qualify people

## Chapter 4: Get Comfortable with Yourself

If you want to become a more persuasive person, you must first get comfortable within your own skin. It's going to be very hard to persuade other people to get on the same page as you when you yourself are feeling conflicted.

If you feel that you're not all that confident or you doubt your capabilities, why should you expect other people to have confidence in what you have to say? Persuasion flows from a solid foundation of confidence.

Now, the good news is that you don't have to have a huge amount of confidence. Even a little can go a long way. As long as you're comfortable with what you have, you will do just fine.

Unfortunately, a lot of unpersuasive people don't bother to do this. They think that persuasion is all about working on somebody else. It's all external. So they focus on the other person, and their efforts fall flat because they don't have a position of strength to work from.

You have to have that inner core of confidence so you would be able to continue to try persuading other people, regardless of how resistant they may seem at first.

Let me tell you, the first few times you try to convince other people, chances are, you will fall flat. In many cases, people just don't want to hear it. In some cases, people would like to get more information. In others, you send conflicting signals and they're confused. Whatever the case may be, the first few times, or even first several hundred times you try to convince people, you may not exactly get the response you're looking for.

Make things easy on yourself by first resolving to get comfortable with yourself. Here are some key pieces of advice that would enable you to do just that.

**Focus on What You Can Learn**

Nothing could make you feel more uncomfortable than thinking that the social interaction that you're going to engage in is some sort of do or die situation. When you paint the next deal or the next presentation in a desperate light, you're putting all sorts of negative pressure on yourself.

Please understand that pressure, in and of itself, is not a bad thing. You can push yourself to a higher level of performance if you apply positive pressure. This is why it's a good idea to focus on what you can learn.

When you know you're going to get into some sort of social interaction, don't focus on what you stand to gain, how important the deal is, how badly you need to meet your quota, or how much you desire a member of the opposite sex. Instead, focus on what you can learn. This makes it fun. It makes the whole process less intimidating.

When you adopt a learning attitude, setbacks don't look like defeats. They don't look like humiliations. They don't look like anything negative at all. Instead, you expect them because you're learning. So focus on what you can learn.

## Focus on Your Curiosity About New People

When you approach any kind of interpersonal situation out of curiosity, you are less scared and intimidated. This can go a long way in making you feel more comfortable.

When you nurture and cultivate your own natural sense of curiosity about other people, social interactions are not as scary. Sure, there's a lot at stake. Maybe you're trying to get a contract, maybe you're trying to get a deal going, but when you approach this from a sense of curiosity, you actually become more effective.

Why? People can see your comfort level. You're actually interested in who they are as a person outside and apart from whatever you can get out of them. Your curiosity makes you more comfortable.

You're not there to impress people. You're not there to get something. Instead, you're there because you truly want to know more about them. This not only sets them at ease and increases their comfort level, it also increases yours.

In fact, you can create an upward spiral of mutual reactions. When they see that you're comfortable, they get more comfortable. When you see that they're comfortable and at ease, you become more comfortable and more effective. Do you see how this works?

## Focus on How You Can Help Others

One of the golden rules of salesmanship says that to get what you want, you must first give other people what they're looking for.

A lot of rookie salespeople mess this up because they do the reverse. When they go on a sales call, they focus on the commission they stand to make. That's their entire focus. How much is this deal worth? What do I stand to gain if I get this account? It is no surprise that rookie salespeople don't do all that well.

You have to remember that people are smarter than you give them credit for. When a sales prospect sees that you're looking at the deal primarily based on how you can benefit from it, they become uncomfortable.

However, when you approach the interaction based on what you can contribute and how you can help others, you look less desperate. You look more comfortable and confident, and this makes them comfortable around you. This paves the way for a greater connection and higher levels of persuasion.

## Don't Focus on What You Stand to Get From Others

There are many ways you can gain from other people. I'm not just talking about money. You can gain based on the doors they can open for you. You can benefit from your connections based on the introductions that they can make. They can lead you to certain resources.

The problem here is, if you come into social interactions based on your need to benefit from others or to get from others, it's easy for you to look uncomfortable. After all, you're putting all this time, effort and energy to get something from somebody.

When you focus instead on what you stand to give, people are more at ease. Also, you are more comfortable because you're no longer feeling that you're doing something that people normally would not want to do.

Normally, people don't want to give. People would rather take. Since you've turned things around and now you are looking to give instead of take, you're more comfortable. You feel that you're not doing something out of the ordinary. You're doing something based on your own terms and based on your own agenda which you have chosen to give.

Again, when you're comfortable, you set people around you at ease. They're less likely to put up a fight. They're less likely to put up a defense. You're able to communicate more clearly.

This should be your focus. Take your mind away from what you stand to extract or get from others.

## Don't Think in Terms of Win/Lose

Another reason why people fail with persuasion is because they go into a situation, assuming that the only way they can gain from that interaction is if the other person loses out at some level or another.

If that is your attitude, then you're going to carry yourself in a way where you look grasping or manipulative. At the very least, you would come off as somebody who has some sort of ulterior motive or hidden agenda. These are not exactly comforting signals to people around you.

Instead of being embraced with open arms and being given the benefit of the doubt, people would have more than healthy levels of skepticism about your motives. Don't be surprised if they put up their guard and try to filter out your motivations.

This doesn't create a comfortable environment. People are on edge. There's tension in the air. All this flows from your mindset.

If you think that you're there to win at their expense, then you're playing the game wrong. You're sending off the wrong signals because you are tense. You're out there to dominate, extract, take or get.

Turn things around and think in terms of win/win. You're there to look at opportunities with them so they gain and you gain. Even better, assume the attitude that you're there to give. And the positive "side effect" of this is that both of you stand to gain.

## Practice the Worst Case Scenario Coping Game

To get comfortable in an unfamiliar situation, you have to overcome your fears of failure. Let's face it, ending up with pie on your face or embarrassing yourself are not exactly pleasant scenarios.

However, you need to understand that these things do happen. Even the best laid plans sometimes go wrong. Do not be so afraid of things going south that you end up sabotaging yourself.

You don't want to put yourself in a position where you go into a social interaction so fearful of failure that you look so uncomfortable that you make others uncomfortable around you. People do this all the time.

To short-circuit that fear, you need to do the following. You need to ask yourself: What is the worst thing that can happen?

You can apply this to almost all social situations. You can be approaching very attractive members of the opposite sex, you can be preparing for a sales meeting that may be worth millions of dollars, you may be preparing for a job interview or an interview for the top spot in your company.

These are high pressure situations. But don't let the fact that there's a tremendous amount of pressure and big stakes involved turn up the pressure on you. You have to have some healthy distance between the consequences of the meeting or interaction and your perception of your value as a human being.

One of the most effective ways to deal with this is to think about the worst case scenario. If things go south, what's the worst thing that can happen? It turns out that it's not as bad as you think.

For example, if you are applying for the top job in your company, what's the worst thing that can happen? That's right, you end up where you currently are.

Maybe you're a vice president shooting for the CEO spot. If you fail in that pressure cooker interview environment, what happens? That's right, you get back to your job. You get back to your current position. It's not like they can fire you.

Similarly, if you see somebody who's really, really attractive and you want to get their number, possibly meet up later on, what's the worst thing that can happen? She can say "no." Has anything been taken away from you? Have you been fundamentally changed prior to you asking her out or asking for her contact information?

Of course, not. You just go back to where you are. In fact, this is the most common answer to the "worst case scenario" question.

Take comfort from this fact. You're not losing anything. Whatever you lose is something that you made up for yourself.

You may have set yourself up to feel ugly, unattractive, unappealing and worthless because a really good looking woman turned you down. But that's just all in your head. You are exactly the same person after you got rejected as the person you were before you asked the question. Do you see how this works?

Believe it or not, this answer keeps cropping up again and again when you ask yourself, "What is the worst case scenario?" Take comfort from this. Be comfortable about the fact that the worst thing that can happen is you go back to where you were before.

## Focus on What You've Already Achieved

Part of preparing for any kind of social interaction involves taking realistic stock of what you have to work with. You'd be surprised as to how much you have. You're not exactly the complete and total loser that you may think you are. You've got a lot to work with.

The longer the list you make in your mind, the stronger the message becomes. This message can really be boiled down to one sentence: *I am worthy*.

This can take many different forms: I've succeeded before, I've gotten the numbers of very attractive women before, I've made a lot of money before, I've gotten good grades before. On and on it goes. But it all goes back to the same place: "*I am worthy.*"

Make sure to do this. And most importantly, take comfort from this.

You have to understand that your fears are only as big as you make them. And believe me, one of the biggest ways to blow up the size of your fears is to reduce the size of your present achievements.

**Keep It Natural**

When you've started talking in a presentation or you've started your approach in a social setting, keep things natural. The key here is to maintain a sense of urgency. This is urgent. This is important. This is serious.

But it has to look natural. This means that you let your words flow. You draw on your inner comfort level, so you look like you're not desperate nor frustrated. If you're able to do this with an appropriate level of urgency, you become a more persuasive person.

Persuasive people are confident people. They draw this confidence from the comfort they feel inside.

When people can detect your confidence, guess what happens? They're drawn to you. How come? They, too, at some level or another, lack confidence. That's why they would like to absorb your confidence.

Let's put it this way, when given a choice between people who are comfortable in their own skin and who are confident, and other people who lack confidence and look pained and pressured, people would rather deal with confident individuals.

Several scientific studies bear out the important connection between internal comfort levels and confidence, and persuasion skills and influence.

In a 2008 research study done in Carnegie Mellon University in Pittsburgh, Pennsylvania, four test participants went through eight rounds where they were asked to buy advice from one of four sources. These sources were volunteers for the study.

Test participants were shown pictures of photographs and they were asked to guess the weight of these people. If they made the right guess, they would get cash. They can buy advice from one of four people regarding the weight of the person in the photo.

The study participants who were asked to guess can see in advance the track record of the people they can buy advice from. They can see how often these advisers guessed correctly.

From the beginning of the study, confident and outgoing advisers were selected more often than insecure or less than confident advisers. When the track record of the advisers were changed to reflect that the confident advisers were often wrong, the study participants who had to make a guess still bought more advice from them.

This 2008 study led by Don Moore, demonstrated that confident and comfortable people are more likely to be persuasive despite the fact that others know their poor track record. Remember, the participants who were asked to guess knew the track record of the people they were buying advice from. But despite this, they still preferred confident people.

When you choose to be comfortable within your own skin and take comfort from your past achievements or your capabilities, you appear more confident. And this makes you more persuasive.

In another study out of Ohio State University in Columbus, Ohio, four groups of test participants were surveyed. There were a total of 12 participants altogether, broken down into four groups of three people. The groups were asked to produce a marketing campaign for products they're supposed to promote.

They were asked before they implemented their marketing campaign if they believed they will be successful. The experiment found that the initial impression of each team about their chances of success played a big role in how their marketing campaign actually performed. In other words, the confident teams were the ones that launched successful marketing campaigns.

Your cognition and confidence in what you're doing has a big impact on your ability to persuade people. Remember, marketing is all about persuasion. You're trying to persuade people to buy your product instead of another product. This study was published in 2002.

With that let's proceed to use your body language towards becoming more persuasive.

# Chapter 5: Controlling Body Language

Did you know that over 90% of human to human communication is nonverbal? That's right. You don't have to use your words or your mouth to communicate.

In fact, in many cases, despite what's coming out of your mouth and whatever sounds you're making, people are still able to see through what you're saying. How come? Your body language gives you away.

People talk a good game and make all sorts of claims, but one look at the total package of nonverbal communications they send with their bodies as well as their tone of voice and how they're speaking may tell a completely different story. Don't overlook the role body language plays in persuasion.

Please understand that you're always sending signals. A little bit of mindfulness goes a long way. Here are some important tips on how to use body language to make yourself to become more persuasive.

## DON'T MAKE IT HARD ON YOURSELF

Before you open your mouth, be mindful of the signals you're sending with your body. Don't make it hard on yourself to communicate.

You're going to be saying stuff to the people in front of you. You're going to try to change their minds. You're going to try to rally them. You're going to attempt to get them to do what you'd like them to do.

Unfortunately, your body might be sabotaging you. Make sure you don't do the following so you don't make things unnecessarily harder on yourself.

### *Don't Cross Your Arms*

When you cross your arms, you come off as defensive. Maybe you don't really believe in what you're saying. Maybe you think you're going to be attacked because you're saying something that you feel people are not going to accept.

Also, when you cross your arms, you look inaccessible. Maybe you're trying to hide something. Maybe you think you are better than the people around you or you think you're smarter. Whatever the case may be, uncross your arms.

### Turning Your Back

At no point in your interaction with another person should you turn your back unless you're telling a story. They will get it if you turn your back as part of a story. But if you are just talking to them and you're trying to convince them of something or you're just trying to get them comfortable, never turn your back.

When you turn your back, you signal disrespect. You signal the impression that they don't really matter as much or you're not really placing much importance in what they have to say or on their feelings.

### Lowering Your Jaw and Giving Them a Look with the Side of Your Eyes or the Side of Your Face

Generally speaking, when you lower your jaw and your jaw is near your chest and you look at people from the top of your bra or through the side of your head, you are signaling hostility. You come off as angry or upset. If you pair this with a smile, it would look really devious. Maybe you have something up your sleeve.

This does not make you look trustworthy. If you give this look, people can get the impression that you're not to be trusted. They can't turn their back on you because they don't want to get backstabbed.

### Do Not Scratch Your Head

When you're talking to somebody and you're trying to gain their trust or persuade them to do something, don't scratch your head. I understand, it may be very itchy, but don't do it. How come? You look unprepared. In fact, if you do it enough, you would look uncomfortable and insecure.

As we have learned in the previous chapter, people gravitate towards confident people. If you're comfortable in your own skin and you take comfort in your capabilities and natural capacity, you project confidence. People would like to be around you. They're more likely to give you the benefit of the doubt.

Well, you send the opposite message with your body when you end up scratching your head. There are variations of this. You can be wiping your face, or maybe you're sweating so you're wiping sweat off your brow. Whatever the case may be, this throws them off.

You either look unprepared, untrustworthy, incompetent, or not all that confident. None of these situations are good. Be mindful of what you're doing with your hands at all times.

### Do Not Put Your Hands in Your Pockets

If you put your hands in your pockets while you're talking to somebody, this looks like you're trying to hide something. You're not showing them your true intention.

Similarly, it can be seen as a sign of insecurity. Maybe you're on the fence. You haven't quite made up your mind. It also signals a lack of confidence.

Depending on how deep you put your hands in your pockets, it might even seem like you're protecting your genitals. Don't laugh. This actually happens. And it's often interpreted in the most negative way.

You're not making a good impression when you put your hands in your pockets, especially if you are speaking to a large group of people.

## KEY BODY SIGNALS YOU NEED TO SEND FOR MAXIMUM PERSUASION

Now that you have a clear idea of not what to do, here are some body signal tips you need to understand to maximize the impact you make on other people.

### *Show Your Palms*

When you are making a point, show your palms. When you do this, you communicate three very important messages. First of all, you're telling people, "You can trust me. I'm not holding anything. I'm not hiding anything. You can see where I'm coming from."

Next, when your palms are up in the air, you draw people's attention to your face and to your upper torso. You are more likely to get your message across because you have their attention.

Finally, when you assume that pose of showing your palms and moving them around, you are able to connect the pacing of your voice with your body motions. This operates on a somewhat hypnotic level. It's very subtle if you don't overdo it, but it does get the point across. You're more likely to get the person that you're talking to on the same page as you.

### *Show Your Neck*

When you're talking to somebody and you show them your neck by craning forward, you are actually showing confidence. How come? In the natural world, when an animal extends its neck, it is showing vulnerability. This is why most animals don't extend their necks. They usually keep it low.

When you do this, people get the message loud and clear: you are a confident person. Otherwise, you wouldn't be doing this because it puts you in a physically vulnerable position. This could show dominance, but usually it shows vulnerability.

When you do this, this means you're telling people, "You can trust me. I have nothing to hide. I don't have my defenses up. I am very weak right now." In other words, "I am very approachable. I have nothing I'm guarding against."

### *Lean Back with Your Hands in a "Pyramid" Shape*

If you're in a social setting and you are sitting down, you might want to lean back with your hands in a pyramid shape. When you assume this position, you signal to the people around you that you are a careful thinker, that you don't do things rashly, and that you are operating from a position of strength and confidence.

These are very attractive features to people. If given a choice, they'd rather not deal with people who lack confidence, who look unprepared, and who look like they're operating under a tremendous amount of pressure.

By simply leaning back with your hands in a pyramid shape or with your hands behind the back of your neck and you clasp your fingers together, you are signalling to people around you that you are relaxed and are in control of the situation. This is very subtle, but it draws attention and it draws confidence.

### *Speak with No Barriers to Your Chest*

When you're speaking to people with your chest wide open without your arms crossed or some sort of artificial barrier in front of you and the person you're connecting to, you come off as more sincere. They feel that they can reach you and that you're not hiding anything. This goes a long way in getting people to feel comfortable around you, which leads to higher levels of persuasion.

### Talk to People with Both of Your Feet Pointed at Them

Let's get one thing clear, people like to feel that they matter. People like to feel that they are important. And let me tell you, nothing makes people feel that you're not taking them seriously when you're talking to them, but your body is positioned towards the door or positioned at an angle where you're not really pointing to them directly.

Make sure that both of your feet are pointed to the person you're talking to and your chest is pointed to them. This communicates, in no uncertain terms, that your ears are open to them. They have your attention.

This makes you more persuasive because this fosters a genuine communication exchange. You're not screwing around. You are signalling respect. You're making them feel that you are paying attention to them and that they matter to you.

### Keep Your Body Open to Your Contact

By making sure that your chest is flat or you lean slightly forward as somebody is talking, you keep your body open to that person. This has the effect of saying, "I am listening to you. You are important to me. You have my full attention."

As I've mentioned above, people like to feel that they matter. If you give off the signal that you don't take them seriously or that they are not all that important to you, they're going to reciprocate. They're going to say, "Well, if I'm not your top priority, then you're not going to be my top priority. I'll find somebody else who will give me the importance and respect that I'm due."

Do you see how this works? Don't let your body signals defeat the words coming out of your mouth. Set them at ease with your presentation and your speech. Make sure you send consistent body language signals.

### *Intentional or Unintentional: It Doesn't Matter*

One of the most common objections I get regarding body language is that it's unintentional. You know what? People couldn't care less about your intent. All they care about is what you actually do with your body and whether you keep your word. Everything else can take a hike.

This is why it's really important to be mindful. Because if you are on a sales call and you're up against another sales person who is very intentional with their body signals and watches their words very carefully, you're operating at a serious disadvantage if you allow yourself to be guided by your intentions.

It doesn't matter whether the signals you send are intentional or unintentional. What matters is how other people will perceive you.

Please remember that people are constantly reading you, so make sure you send the right signals. They couldn't care less about whatever excuse you come up with. They don't care that you may have gotten in an accident or somebody you know may have died. None of that matters. What matters is whether you performed when you needed to perform.

## Body Language Enables You to Become More Persuasive

The final word about body language's impact on persuasion is that it all boils down to removing perceived boundaries and limitations. That's really what it all boils down to.

When you don't sabotage yourself by lowering your jaw, scratching your head, putting your hands in your pockets, turning your back, crossing your arms, you tell people that you're open to them. That you want to communicate with them. You enhance this by showing your palms, your neck, leaning back with your hands in a pyramid shape, making sure that there are no barriers to your chest and making sure both of your feet are pointed to the person you're talking to.

Remember, people are more perceptive than you give them credit for. They might not be able to articulate why they chose one sales person over another or one job applicant over another, but they are sure about their decision. They might not be able to put the reasons into precise words, but they can recognize the feelings and emotional states they experienced.

Conduct yourself for maximum persuasion. Don't overlook or ignore the power and role body language plays in helping you become a more persuasive person.

# Chapter 6: Get People Comfortable Around You

Make no mistake, even if you have mastered body language and have achieved a high level of internal comfort, you still have to communicate all of that. What I mean by this is that there's a reason why you're trying to send the right body language signals and why you're trying to appear confident.

There's a point to all of this, and guess what? It's not about you. Instead, it's about the people around you. These are the people you're trying to impress, these are the people you're trying to persuade, these are the people you are trying to connect to.

If you are unable to get them to feel comfortable around you, then all the body language mastery and internal comfort levels you have managed to achieve will be worthless. Remember, persuasion is all about reaching out to other people.

Follow the tips below to maximize the comfort zone you generate around you in your social interactions.

## Remember: Conversations are Not Interrogations

How many times have somebody told you, "Hey, how're you doing?" People who know how the game works know that this is not really intended to get info from you. You're only supposed to say something fairly superficial and move on.

Conversations are intended to establish mutual comfort. They are not meant to dig for deep information. They are meant to set the tone for your interaction instead of triggering each other to open up deep and hidden truths.

Now, please understand that there will be opportunities for that later on and in different settings. However, most of the time, small talk and medium level conversations are not interrogations. You still have to listen to their answers, but the key here is to establish comfort.

A lot of people get their wires crossed. They think that if they are asked certain questions that they have to really go deep. And instead of setting other people at ease, it has the opposite effect. It actually makes people uncomfortable. It makes the exchange awkward. Don't do that.

## Communicate to Set Others at Ease

How exactly do you communicate so that people will lower their guard? Remember, it's very hard to persuade people when they are suspicious and skeptical of you. When they have their defenses up, it's going to be almost impossible to get them on the same page as you.

These are fairly simple techniques, and you probably already know that. Still, you cannot overlook these because they can go a long way in helping you become more persuasive.

## Remember to Smile

The conventional wisdom is that it takes more facial muscles to frown than it is to smile. The implication is, it's easier to smile. Why don't you do it more often?

A lot of people are under the impression that if they smile, they're somehow losing something, that they're giving themselves away, or that they may look weak or put themselves at some sort of disadvantage. Get those ideas out of your head.

Even if you don't like the person in front of you, smile naturally. When you smile, you speak from the heart. You speak from a place of comfort and confidence.

If you have a tough time smiling, look deep down inside and ask yourself: What are the things do I take pride in? What are the things that I'm thankful for? What are the things that I have managed to achieve in my life? What are the things that I am proud of?

And when you become aware of them, respond with a smile. When you smile, you are responding out of gratitude.

If you're able to do this and you send this signal, it disarms people. They get the message. This is not a fight, this is not a competition. You are a human being, and there's nothing to be upset or to be overly defensive about.

In primate studies, smiling has been linked to tension diffusion. When alpha males come into contact with beta or subordinate males, there's a lot of smiles all around. The alpha isn't smiling, but everybody else is smiling. And this reduces the tension.

Smile more often. It will help you become more persuasive because you lower everybody's guard.

**Find a Conversation Piece**

After you introduce yourself or after you exchange pleasantries, try to find a conversation piece. Maybe they're wearing something or maybe they've said something. Maybe they got a new haircut. Whatever the case may be, communicate that you notice them.

Remember, people like to be made to feel that they matter. People like to feel important. People like to feel that they are worthy of notice. So when you see certain details and you point those out, they feel that you are actually paying attention to them.

Guess what? This makes you look really good in their eyes. This is especially true if they lack confidence or they have low self esteem.

Normally, they may feel that they don't matter all that much. Maybe they think that they're just another face in the crowd, and then here you come and you notice them. How do you think that will make you look in their eyes? You look like a hero.

Now, here's the thing. When you find a conversation piece that is closely connected to them, the key is not to interrogate them. Sure, you'd like to get more details where they got that necklace – maybe it looks like some sort of Mayan or Incan relic, maybe you are genuinely interested in the history behind that necklace – but prepare yourself for a short explanation or no explanation at all.

Maybe they'll just say thank you. Be prepared to accept their answer. Because if you keep digging deeper and deeper, you come across as an interrogator rather than somebody who they can relax around.

Remember, the whole point here is to use conversation pieces to get them to relax. You're trying to get them to feel comfortable around you.

**Get Them to Tell a Story**

Often times, when you find a conversation piece or a point of conversation with somebody, this often prompts them to tell a story.

Most people don't have a problem telling stories because hey, let's face it, a lot of us would like to have our time in the spotlight. We love to talk about ourselves. But if you come across somebody who doesn't want to take the initiative of telling stories about themselves or putting themselves front and center, you need to take the lead.

So when you find a conversation piece and they say "thank you," you can just say, "I have a necklace like that as well" or "My wife picked it up when we went to Machu Pichu." This draws them into your world. You tell them a story. You tell them a little bit about yourself.

And what do you think happens? Reciprocity happens. They can't help but repay you with their own personal story. Repeat this enough times and you get them to relax.

## Get Them to Laugh

Make no mistake about it, one of the best forms of social lubrication is laughter. Because when people are laughing, good-heartedly mind you, not in mocking terms, they have their guard down. This especially true if they're laughing at a situation, not at a person or, worse yet, you.

There's a certain universal aspect to laughter. We share a vulnerable moment when we laugh together. We also express key parts of ourselves, like our sense of humor, our values, what we find important, and so on and so forth.

Also, when you get people to laugh through a funny story or some observational humor, you create a common experience. These are the building blocks of friendships. If you look back at experiences you had with your friends, your friendships deepened when you had shared experiences.

It doesn't matter how old you get, when you have a reunion, don't be surprised if somebody brings up the story. And it reaffirms the bond that you've created when you went through that joint experience together.

The same dynamic applies when you get people to laugh. Now, it's not as powerful as going on a long journey together or going through a tough time together, like if you were in the army together, but any kind of joint experience strengthens bonds.

## The Secret to Comfortable Communications

The secret to mutual comfort is actually pretty straightforward. The more comfortable people get around you, the less defensive they are. This is a big deal because when they don't have their defenses up and they are more likely to give you the benefit of the doubt, they are more suggestible.

Do not abuse this trust. Be mindful of what you say. Make sure that you are able to back up everything you say and make sure that you are able to keep whatever promises you make. This is a tremendous responsibility.

You have to remember that most of the time, people will only choose to be vulnerable around you once. Screw that up and that's the only chance you will ever get. In fact, if things turn out badly, they might have a very negative impression of you.

This is a tremendous responsibility. You're getting people comfortable for mutual benefit. You're not doing this to exploit, you're not doing this for any kind of antisocial purpose, you're doing this for some sort of mutual win-win benefit. Or at least you should.

**Tie Mutual Comfort to Persuasion**

If you are able to increase people's level of comfort around you, they are more likely to give you the benefit of the doubt. This will then enable you to connect with them in a clear and direct way.

When you're making a proposal, tie it to emotional benefits, not features. This is a common rookie mistake sales people make. When they get the prospect comfortable around them, they launch into a product pitch.

Guess what? They couldn't care less about any of that. All they care about is whether the product will deliver benefits or not.

But here's the problem, the benefits they're looking for are inherently emotional, so you have to phrase it in emotional human terms, not cold, mechanical or statistical terms. You also have to tie your proposal to their objectives.

When people are buying a house, they're not looking to buy something that has four walls that looks good. They're buying a container for their memories. They're buying an emotional anchor.

Understand what their real objectives are and tie your proposal to those. Make them the center of your proposal. This requires skill. This requires patience. This requires the willingness to be comfortable and learn from the person in front of you.

You're studying them and you're watching everything you say so that everything revolves around them. And the foundation to all of this happening is a mutual level of comfort.

In a 2015 study out of the University College London, two student groups were examined by a council in a lecture. One group of students was assigned to a strict councilor. The students were not very responsive to this person. The second group of students were assigned to a councilor who cracked jokes and told stories. Compared to the first group of students, the second group were highly engaged, laughing and calm around the councilor. They were also sharing their own personal stories.

This study although statistically small, suggests that people are more comfortable when efforts are made to get them to laugh. Laughing eases social tension and opens people up to deeper levels of engagement. Make no mistake, if you are able to make people around you laugh, this makes things so much easier as far as your powers of persuasion are concerned.

Similarly, in a 2017 study out of Oregon State University, conducted by researcher Michael D. Jones, published in the journal Nature, people were shown footages of several celebrities telling stories regarding vaccines. These seven people were more persuaded by pro-vaccine messages that involves some sort of storytelling. They weren't swayed by technical or statistical information and weren't impressed by scientific data. Instead, when these information was presented in story form, people sat up and paid attention. This study highlights the fact that if you are able to tell stories to the people you're trying to persuade, they are suggestable. They open up to you.

Understand that the statistical and scientific information you're sharing with them is not what convinces them. Instead, it's how you frame this information in the form of a story. People are able to relate better on a personal level. This increases persuasive ability.

# Chapter 7: Build Trust with the Right Storytelling

Make no mistake, human beings understand the world in terms of stories. Let me put it this way, every single second you're picking up all sorts of stimuli form the external world. These are the things that you see, hear, touch, taste, and smell.

Interestingly enough, out of the things, the things that you choose to focus on, you only remember a small part. When you remember these materials, you fit it into your personal narrative. This is the ongoing story about yourself that forms a key art of your identity. This is how people navigate and make sense of the world. It's one great story.

Interestingly enough, the stories that we tell ourselves determine our lives. For instance, if you view yourself as an unattractive person who brings out the worst in everybody, how successful do you think you will be? Chances are either you would detect conflict or you would contribute to it because that is your mindset. On the other hand, if you see yourself as always being part of the solution and as some sort of positive voice in a community you find yourself in, you probably would have differ results. That's how important your personal narrative is.

Personal narrative is a key part of your identity. But if you unravel it, it really is made up of stories. Stories help make sense of otherwise complex situations. But stories are never neutral. We always choose them. They may not seem like a choice because we've grown accustomed to selecting certain types of stories instead of others, but there ultimately they are still choices. They always trigger emotions.

Be aware of the stories you keep telling yourself. Your personal stories explain your lack of success, frustrations, and insecurities in life. They also explain your victories, achievements, hopes, and dreams.

Unfortunately, most people refuse to see their personal stories as voices. It is very tempting for many people to assume that their stories are simply something they were born with. This is not true. You can always choose your stories and which to tell. At the very least, tell the right stories.

When you're trying to persuade other people, first, these stories must be personal. If you tell a story that is very distant, somewhat cold, or even mechanical or lifeless, people are not going to be drawn in. They might think it's interesting but ultimately, their interest level will fall off. But if you tell a story that makes the listener feel that you're "letting them in" on a secret or some sort of truth that isn't well known about you, they feel a stronger emotional connection to you. In fact, they feel compelled at some level or another to respond to your personal story with their own personal story. A little bit of vulnerability goes a long way.

When you tell a personal story and you give people opportunities to share their story, you're also triggering a need that almost everybody has. What is this need? Feeling special. Everybody craves the spotlight. Don't let anybody trick you into thinking that they could care less about anybody's attention. They're just fooling themselves. Most people crave some sort of attention.

When you let people tell their story or prompt them to tell their stories because you opened the door with your own, you make them feel that they matter. You end up making them feel validated and in turn, will make you look attractive and trustworthy in their eyes. At least there more open to you.

Telling the right stories involve narratives that contain universal elements. I know this seems like really heavy duty philosophical stuff, so let me break it down. What unites people? You think it's our tough guy persona or our victories, no. What unites us are things like pain, loss, triumph, discover, and humor. Focus on those. Included those on your stories.

## Tell interesting stories

I don't expect you to master this the first time you try it. But when you're telling stories to become more persuasive, keep repeating the same stories with different crowds and pay attention to their reaction. Sooner or later you will get this right.

Generally interesting stories have funny endings, twists, or some sorts of obvious interpretation that gives people a laugh. This is very important because you don't want to tell a sad story to people you just met.

I went to a dinner party in San Francisco one time and I came across this person who told me that she was sexually abused when she was 8 years old. It hit me like a ton of bricks. I just met this person, we were having a good time, we were laughing, there are other people around and then all of a sudden she dropped this revelation on me. I didn't quite know how to respond.

My reaction is pretty much universal. People are not prepared for such heavy revelations. So when you're telling a story, make sure that it is interesting enough but in a positive way. You want people to have a positive impression on you. You don't want to make them feel heavy, burned or weighed down. Regardless of how you do it, make sure that you tell your story in an authentic way.

If you're sharing a vulnerable part of you involving some sort of pain or loss, but of course ending with something funny or whimsical, authenticity is the key. The moment you come off as practiced, polished, or rehearsed, people lose interest. In fact, that's the most positive response you will get. You don't want negative response.

What's the worst response you would get? Well, people might feel betrayed or feel that you just played or deceived them. Instead of making a friend, you just might have made an enemy. At the very least this person might talk negatively behind your back. Don't give people that impression. Authenticity is the key.

## The right stories make you more human

When there's a nice blend of universal human elements like pain, loss, triumph, discovery, and humor in your story, along with a funny ending or an unexpected turn of events, you look more human. It becomes so much easier for the people you're talking to, to relate with you. They find it easier to identify with you.

Once you are able to achieve this, it doesn't take much effort to gain their trust. How come? There are so many different people and so many potential connections out there, but since you're the one who opened up to them with a story and are able to relate to them on a "one to one" basis, they feel that you're authentic and they can't help but be drawn to you. I'm not talking about of any kind of physical or emotional attracting, I'm talking about seeing you in a different light than other people.

This is a tremendous competitive advantage. You are more persuasive in this context because when somebody feels this way about you, they are more likely to give you the benefit of doubt. The theme of your story opens up to the argument that you are making or the thesis of your proposal. In other words when you set people at ease with story after story, it becomes easier for you to tie everything in with the thesis of your proposal.

You have to do this right. You don't want to come off as a manipulative salesman. You'd end up sabotaging yourself if you did that. But still, it's really important to make sure that the stories have a common theme. It's not like your just spitting out story after story with no apparent logical connection between them. This might make for great conversations, but it really would go nowhere because you're not really calling the shots here.

There has to be a purpose to these stories. One is to get people conformable around you. Second, to get people to see you a real flesh and blood human being who is authentic and third, to get people to open up to you with their own stories.

In the research I mentioned in chapter six, out of the University College London, it also validates the power of storytelling. When the two student groups were assigned to different lectures with different styles, the group assigned to the lecturer who was cracking jokes and telling stories had a more favorable response. They are more likely to open up. The most interesting part of this study is that not only that people are engaged and more open to persuasion, but they are also more likely to volunteer their own personal stories. The connection gets deeper and deeper.

This makes it so much easier to persuade people because you're no longer a stranger or somebody who is some sort of unknown quantity. People are not wondering whether they can trust you or not. They are not deciding whether you keep you out or let you in.

Similarly, in a 2006 study out of Pennsylvania State University, participants were asked to listen to three versions of the same speech. The only difference between these versions involves the placement of the word "damn". Usually, when people hear the world damn, they interpret it as swearing. This is not exactly a pleasant word.

Interestingly enough, when people were asked about their impressions of the three speeches, the version where the word "damn" appeared in the beginning, was viewed more positively. In fact, the seven study participants said that that version of the speech was far more persuasive than the other two. These other version put the word damn either at the end or keep it out entirely.

This study highlights the importance of authenticity. If you're trying to persuade people, often times the best thing you can do is to be completely open with them. Don't try to pretend to be somebody you're not. People are actually very, very smart. They can see through all sorts of charades. If you're trying to put on a show, it's only a matter of time until people discover that you are a phony.

Authenticity is a powerful persuasive tool. But of course, you shouldn't overdo it. There is such a thing as "oversharing". Finally in Stanford's graduate school of business, researcher Jennifer Aaker released a 2016 paper that studied the performance of 25 students. These students were tasked to give a one minute pitch to their class members to persuade them about a certain topic.

Interestingly enough, some one minute pitches include many statistics, others had less. In fact, the average pitch had around 2.5 statistics. Among these, however, was one that had a story. After ten minutes of hearing these different pitches, the researcher overseeing the study requested that the students write down all the ideas from the pitches that they remembered. Shockingly, only 5% of the participants remembered any statistic. However, 63% of them remembered that one pitch that had the story.

This study highlights the importance of stories in terms of recall. Understand that if you're trying to persuade people, at the very least, they must remember what you're trying to persuade them about. If you use stories to make your pitch or to get them to like you, they are more responsive. They are more likely to become more responsive because they have a higher chance of remembering what you said.

# Chapter 8: Unleash the Power of Likeability

Humans are designed by hundreds if not thousands of years of behavioral evolution. Throughout these hundreds of thousands of years, we have learned certain behaviors. One of these behavioral truths is that we are more likely to trust people who are similar to us. With everything else being equal, if you come across a stranger who looked like you, had the same mannerisms as you, talked like you, share the same language, and possibly came from the same religion, chances are you are more likely to like that person.

It is not surprise that people who share the same ethnic, cultural, and class background tend to view each other more favorably than people outside their group. For example, if you are an upper class, living in a certain part of town, and have a certain level of education attainment, you are more likely to at least give another person who came from the some background the benefit of the doubt.

You are more likely to be suspicious and less trusting of people who are completely different from you. Maybe they are working or poor class, or they live at the other side of town, maybe they don't have much education, this is part of human condition. This is hard wired into our DNA.

Believe it or not, if the shoe is on the other foot, the same rules apply. People who are from the working class that have a certain background are not going to feel at home when they come across somebody who is completely different from them. People are more likely to trust others who are similar to them.

Armed with this information, you can make yourself more likeable. The first thing that you need to do to become more likeable is to choose to smile. Depending on your cultural background, smiling may or may not come easy to you. In many parts of Southeast Asia as well as South America and Africa, people smile readily. They smile without prompting. In fact, many cases they simile even when nobody's watching.

However, on other parts of the globe, smiling is actually viewed as a sign of weakness or insecurity. It may even provoke suspicion or distrust. I'm not even going to name the countries that have these interpretation. But here's a hint. They're in colder climates.

When you smile, you signal non-aggression and accessibility. You're not holding people off, you're not blocking them, nor sending off threat signals. You are signaling to people around you, "I am a friendly person."

Next, you can mimic the person in front of you. Look at their mannerisms. Pay attention to their word choice. Look at how they look at you and their posture. Believe it or not, you can get that person to see you in a more favorable light if you copy some of the details that I mentioned above. Don't be surprised as to how they light up when you use their favorite phrase from time to time. The same applies to their posture or their physical orientation.

Another way you can build likeability, is reciprocity. Simply telling people that you're going to give them your time can trigger reciprocity. Most people can understand how precious time is. It is a luxury for most people. The fact that you are taking some time off your business schedule just for them is a big deal. They're more likely to reciprocate. But instead of giving you their time, they're giving you more of their attention and more likely give you the benefit of the doubt.

Another way you can trigger reciprocity is by giving gifts. It does have to be very big. In fact, in a study involving tipping with mints out Monmouth University in 2006, servers who placed a restaurant bill with mints were more likely to get bigger tips than servers only presented the bill alone to diners.

This experiment highlighted the power of reciprocity. People can't help but to repay one good dead with another. As mentioned in the introduction to this chapter, these behaviors are hard wired into our DNA. Our ancestors were more likely to survive all sorts of disasters if they reciprocated one good act for another. This creates mutual survival.

Now can you imagine an individual who did not have this tendency? They just take, take, and take. Well, chances are the social groups they're in are probably not going to like them all that much. It's probably not unlikely that they get kicked out of groups. Those individuals quickly get bred out of the population because they might get eaten by wolves or they might not be able to withstand the elements because they're not plugged into the protection a social unit.

Reciprocity is a big deal. It plays a big role in the science of likeably. Now, some cultures place a bigger value on reciprocity than others. In fact, in Filipino culture, even a little bit of gifting is bred to trigger a debt of obligation, many times bigger than the initial gift.

Another subtle way you can make yourself more likeable is when you engage in recapping. This involves listening to what the persons in front of you is saying and then repeating what they said as a summary. When you do this, you let them know that you are actually listing to them. This is a big deal because people, like I keep repeating in this book, like to feel that they matter. We all like to feel validated.

### Some warnings

Make sure that you don't overdue mimicking. If you do, instead of bonding with the person in front of you, it will come off like you are mocking them. Another note to keep in mind, reciprocity doesn't have to involve physical gifts. Even a symbolic gift or even a compliment is enough. Of course when you're giving compliments to trigger a reciprocity, it must be natural. It also must be backed up by your facial expressions as well as your body language.

When giving a little symbolic or intangible gift, make sure that the value is easy to understand. For example, if you work in a bank and you know that there is a special loan program for certain types of businesses and you come across somebody who runs such a business, simply giving them the information about the social program will make you look like a hero in their eyes. After all, they stand to save a lot of money in interest. Understand that the gift that you gave them is just information. But that information packs a lot of value. Just as importantly, that value is readily apparent to them, they don't have to guess.

### *A little bit of eye contact goes along way*

Whether you're mimicking, smiling, engaging reciprocity or recapping, make sure there is proper eye contact. When you do this, you engage with them with a person to person level. They can see your intentions. They can get an understanding of what you're about. This simply maintaining eye contact turbocharges the likeability actions described above.

In a 2002 study, out of the French Institution UBS, 20 participants were asked to make random requests to random people on the streets. The participants were not given any other instructions. They were supposed to figure things out on their own.

Interestedly enough, of the 20 participants who asked for help from total strangers, the ones who established eye contact are more likely to be successful. What is the secret? It's not just eye contact. They also followed up with the phrase "you're free to decline". In other words, when they make a request for help, they look to the person in the eye and made the request but they followed up quickly with the statement.

This dynamic operated in two levels. First of all, when you look people straight in the eye, it's a human to human connection. You are stopping them because you are giving them a purely personal request. But when you say "you are free to decline", you're giving them a choice. In other words, you are respecting their autonomy. Thanks to this pairing, people are more likely to be persuaded.

In a 2014 study out of Cornell University, 63 students were asked to select among different boxes of cereal that had the same rabbit mascot. All the cereal boxes were the same, except for the eyes of the rabbit mascot. Normally, the mascot is looking at the cereal. Some of the boxes were edited in photo shop to make the rabbit look directly at the observer. Interestingly enough, more of the 63 student survey selected the cereal box where the rabbit was looking directly at them.

This experiment highlighted the importance of eye contact. When you look at people straight in the eye, you communicate to them in a certain level. You are signaling your willingness to connect and you are reaching out. It becomes personal.

# Chapter 9: Take Advantage of Social Proof

Let's get several facts out of the way. First of all, people don't know you from head-up. You're just another face in the crowd. You stepped out of the crowd and now you're talking to them, but they don't know you.

Second, people don't want to get ripped off. People work hard for their money, and they want to hang on to something they worked so hard for. Finally, people use social connections to pre-qualify people they would listen to.

With everything else being equal, you are more likely to go to the accountant your buddy referred you to, than any accountant you found on the internet. It doesn't really matter what kind of materials you have read or how many publications that accountant has authored. Generally speaking, with everything else being equal, people are more likely to go with referrals made by people they already know, trust, and respect. Welcome to the world of social proof.

If you want to be more persuasive, you have to produce some sort of social proof. Generally, this can be done fairly easily. For example if you are selling a product, don't juts say "this product works". You're probably not going to persuade too many people.

Now the dynamic will change if you posted actual testimonials of people who have actually interacted with your product. The more authentic and dynamic the testimonial, the better. In other words, you can post a picture of a person standing next to your product with a thumbs up and that can carry some weight.

You can post the same picture along with written statement of that person talking about how awesome the product is. That's more likely to work. However, if you really want to connect, show a video of the person using the product and then saying in front of the camera, "this was my life before and this is my life now. This product has really helped me."

Social proof works. Here's the problem, a lot of marketers completely blow it with social proof. They use some sort of template or they just simply do it out of context. It is no surprise that there are tons of products out there with sales pages full of testimonials that do not sell. How come? Effective social proof in the form of testimonials use the same context as the people you're trying to persuade.

For example, if you know that the vast majority people who buy your products come from a certain background and have a small set of problems that are pretty much similar across the board, the people in you testimonials must share the same background and same problems. Otherwise, your prospects would watch your video and just move on. They couldn't connect because the people giving the testimonials are not similar enough to them. They cannot see the connection.

In addition to context, you must also use the same type of people. This way the prospects can relate personally to the ones giving the testimonials. You have do a tremendous amount of consumer research here. Are most of your users, female? Then it doesn't make sense to use a man as a video spokesperson. Are mosey of your buyers, college students? Then it doesn't make sense to feature somebody who is in his 50s.

Finally, effective social proof highlights the "before" and "after" states. In other words, the testimonial must showcase the effectiveness of the product by highlighting the change in a real person's life. This packs quite bit of a punch. Otherwise, you're just sprouting out theories. You're just saying to the person watching your video that you have something interesting. It will not be their priority.

When you highlighted somebody who is dealing with the same context and the same situation, demonstrably, benefited because of the clear contrast of what happened to them before and after they used the product, then they would pay attention. You see how this works?

## Provide social proof through group proof

Another way you can provide social proof is through group proof. Testimonials involves individual proofs. These are actual flesh and blood human beings who use the product. With group proof you're talking about aggregating the collective experiences of a larger number roof people. This involves statistics, or group based case studies.

This type of social proof is not personally identifiable. Still it can be quite convincing because you're using the power of numbers. The higher the number, the more "universal" the applicability of your solution. If you said "we surveyed 10 million housewives and 98% of them said our product is the best", your target audience member would probably sit up and pay attention. Ten million is quite a large number.

The other key aspect of social proof: purpose.

Make no mistake, effective social proof also involves socially desired practice. In other words, when you tell people "not only is my product effective, but it fits with society's expectations." In this situation, you are appealing to people's need to conform. Again, just like our discussion in section about likeability, we are hardwired to conform at some level or other. Otherwise, our ancestors would've died out a long time ago.

There are certain evolutionary advantages to confirming to group norms. When you present social proof that lines up you product with certain group expectations, you are appealing to this deep seethed aspect of the human condition.

In a 1978 experiment conducted by Harvard University researchers, experimenters asked people in line for a photocopier, if they can skip ahead of the line. The experimenters asked two set of questions. First, they asked, "Can I use the photocopier?" When they used this question, they were allowed to get to the front of the line 60% of the time.

However, when they used the other question of, "Can I use the photocopier because I have to make some copies?" 93% of the time, people let them get to the head of the line. Pay attention to the second request. Everybody in line obviously wanted to make copies, so on that level, the request didn't really make any sense.

What this experiment shows is that having a reason provides social proof in persuasion. You have to give a reason, and this increases your chances of being persuasive. This reason can be very basic. In fact, it can be a reason that most other people have. That is a form of social proof. The fact that your reason resonates with the people that you're trying to persuade because they have that reason as well is a form of social proof.

# Chapter 10: Pre-qualify Your Audience

If you want to increase your persuasion skills, pre-qualify people. What this means is that you just need to filter people that you are trying to persuade. This is probably one of the first lessons that marketers ever get to learn. Whether you're marketing offline or online, it doesn't matter. If you qualify your prospects, you are more likely to make a sale.

Take the case of credit card customers, a lot of people who call their credit card companies call because they have problems with their billing statement. Maybe they sent in payment and it didn't get credited. Whatever the case may be, when they call, it is a sales opportunity because inbound calls can be dealt with to deal with the primary concern of the caller, but the person can be marketed to for related services.

This is a form of qualification. Similarly, if you are selling stuff online, if you pick keywords that signify intent, there is a higher likelihood that you would convert traffic that you generate with those keywords. For example, you can target the words "Tennis Shoes" all you want, and chances are, you're not going to make much money.

How come? There are so many different people with different motivations and intentions typing in the words "Tennis Shoes" into Google. Some people might be looking for different models. Others are looking for a history of tennis shoes because they're writing a term paper. Even others are simply looking to design a tennis shoe.

Most of these people are not on the market to buy a pair of shoes. Compare that situation with the keywords "Buy Tennis Shoes." There is a high likelihood that people who type "Buy Tennis Shoes" or "I want to buy tennis shoes" into Google are looking to purchase something. Even though the traffic volume of people typing in that search term into Google will be much lower that the people searching for "Tennis Shoes," if you were to target those keywords, you probably will make a lot more money.

Filtered people are easier to persuade. This is why it's a good idea to come up with qualification filters to make your job of persuading your prospects easier.

There are many ways to recognize how people self-filter or qualify themselves for your offer. You can go to certain events. You can go to certain parts of a room. You can go to certain departments in an organization. Believe it or not, people tend to self-segregate. There is a lot of self-filtering going on. If you don't believe me, just go to any campus in the United States.

Different people of different interests hang out together at certain times during the day. The same goes on in the internet. For example, if you're looking to sell tennis shoes, there are forums where people talk about sneakers. If you are looking to offer immigration services for people looking for a visa to enter the United States or Canada, there are specialized forums for that topic.

People self-segregate themselves all the time. This is especially true when it comes to Facebook groups and Facebook pages. You are more likely to persuade people If you are very specific about the groups and pages you post your content on.

In a 2008 study from Northwestern University, researcher Daniel O'Keefe studied 6,378 students. The participants were surveyed regarding skin health. Some messages focused on the negative consequences of neglecting your skin. They emphasized skin cancer. Other messages focused on what you stand to gain if you take good care of your skin. They emphasized getting "attractive skin."

The study was aimed to test whether **people would respond better to negativity over positivity**. For the longest time, a lot of advertising professionals were convinced that if you use scare tactics, you will be able to sell more products. If you dwelt on the negative outcome of certain decisions, you would be able to push people to buy a product to prevent that outcome.

Well, it turned out that most people would rather look at what they stand to gain. They would rather look at the positives of any change you're trying to convince them of making. In other words, it's a good idea to direct your audience towards a better place, instead of scaring them about stuff that they should avoid.

In a 1992 University of Georgia study, 24 couples were studied in the context of relationship therapy. The counselor conducting the interviews noticed that when couples already had an idea of what they expected from their relationship, it was easier for the counselor to give them advice. They were also more likely to follow the advice.

On the other hand, if the couple did not really have a good idea about what they expected from each other or from their relationship, it was so much harder for the counselor to give them any kind of advice. In other words, when people preselect themselves in terms of receptiveness towards some sort of outcome, they are more likely to be persuaded.

# Conclusion

If you want to become a more effective person, you need to invest in your powers of persuasion. Reading this book is the first step. You have to not only read this book and pay attention to its tips, but you have to actually carry it out. You have to understand that persuasion is like a muscle. For you to grow your muscles, you have to apply stress to them.

That's right. You have to apply pressure. It's not going to be pleasant at first because you've grown accustomed to doing things a different way. The good news is, the more you use your powers of persuasion, the more you will be able to connect the dots and things will start getting easier for you.

The hardest part is getting started. But once you've achieved a certain level of momentum, it becomes easier and easier. I wish you nothing but the greatest success in everything you do in life.

**DISCLAIMER**

particular purpose. No warranty may be created or extended by sales or promotional materials. The advice and recipes contained herein may not be suitable for everyone. This work is sold with the understanding that the author is not engaged in rendering medical, legal or other professional advice or services. If professional assistance is required, the services of a competent professional person should be sought. The author shall not be liable for damages arising here from. The fact that an individual, organization of website is referred to in this work as a citation and/or potential source of further information does not mean that the author endorses the information the individual, organization to website may provide or recommendations they/it may make. Further, readers should be aware that Internet websites listed in this work might have changed or disappeared between when this work was written and when it is read.

Adherence to all applicable laws and regulations, including international, federal, state, and local governing professional licensing, business practices, advertising, and all other aspects of doing business in any jurisdiction in the world is the sole responsibility of the purchaser or reader.